CELEBRATING
WRITERS

WRITERS

From Possibilities
Through Publication

Ruth **Ayres**
with Christi **Overman**

 Stenhouse
PUBLISHERS

www.stenhouse.com

Portland, Maine

Stenhouse Publishers
www.stenhouse.com

Library of Congress Cataloging-in-Publication Data
Ayres, Ruth, 1977-
   Celebrating writers : from possibilities through publication / Ruth Ayres with Christi Overman.
      pages cm
   Includes bibliographical references.
   ISBN 978-1-57110-950-7 (pbk. : alk. paper) -- ISBN 978-1-62531-000-2 (ebook) 1. Creative writing. 2. Authorship--Technique. I. Overman, Christi. II. Title.
   PN189.A96 2013
   808.02--dc23
                                                                2013021001

Cover design, interior design, and typesetting by designboy creative.

Manufactured in the United States of America

PRINTED ON 30% PCW
RECYCLED PAPER

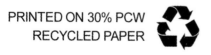

19 18 17 16 15 14 13   9 8 7 6 5 4 3 2 1

To **Joy Goshert**,
who empowers me to celebrate.
—RA

To the **Original Superkiddos**,
without whom this book would not exist.
—CO

Contents

Acknowledgments

Ruth:

Some days I think I need to be pinched to believe I'm actually a writer. To get to write about celebration and joy in the writing process makes me think I need a double pinch. The thing is, none of it would be possible if it weren't for the support, love, and sometimes a kick in the pants from some special people. My joy runs deep.

The huge online network of blog readers and Twitter and Facebook users who constantly give more than I can give back. A special thank you to Stacey Shubitz, who stepped with me into cyberspace many years ago.

Bill Varner and the Stenhouse crew for believing in me.

Franki Sibberson for being excited about my writing even when I wasn't.

Brenda Power and Heather Rader for their continual encouragement and reading of drafts.

Christi Overman and her class of Original Superkiddos for welcoming me into their community. Christi, it was joyful to plan this book together with you.

The staff and students at Wawasee Community Schools for showing joy and letting me use your stories to inspire others.

The Wawasee Middle School writing group, Rebecca Nguyen, Shelley Kunkle, Tam Hess, Dave Eldridge, Dave Palmer, Andrea Komorowski, Sarah Stoelting, and Carla Winegardner, for reminding me that writing together always brings people closer.

The members of my writing group, Ruth Metcalfe, Mary Helen Gensch, Tam Hess, and Tammy Schultz, who encourage me to be a light-hearted writer and convince me my words matter.

Friends like the Stout, Shock, Stan, and Holst families for helping me keep my eyes on the things that matter most.

Deb Gaby, fellow instructional coach, copresenter, colleague, and, most importantly, a true friend, for listening, laughing, celebrating, and putting some words on the page.

My parents, Pam and Kevin Myers, who make me hot tea and a stop-and-go breakfast on the days I'm late because I stayed up writing past bedtime.

Andy, who makes me laugh instead of cry.

Hannah, for learning to make a perfect cup of coffee and bring it to me without spilling.

Stephanie for forcing me to take breaks and play catch in the yard.

Jordan for a smile that makes me smile.

Sam for Saturday morning "Mom and Sam Time." You are my favorite writing partner *in the universe*.

"The joy of the Lord is my strength" (Nehemiah 8:10).

Christi:

There are etchings on my heart from a few lovely people.

Evan, really, there are no words. Nothing that I say here or anywhere could express my thankfulness for you.

Mom and Dad, now that I'm a grown-up and I am making all these steps through life, I can trace every one of my good decisions back to you.

Jon, you really are the best brother I could ask for. As a kid, I demanded that you do lots of things, many of which you refused to do (thank goodness). Now I know I could ask you to do anything and you'd do it. Are you up for reading my book?

Ruth, thank you for believing in me, not only as a friend, but as a colleague and fellow writer. I'm so glad our names are forever together in this book.

Cheryl Conroy and Barb Bean, thank you for all those times you took me by the hand and showed me by your examples how to teach well, stand up for what's right, and to laugh always. Thank you for all the countless hugs after I rushed to your rooms crying, for loaning precious books to me, and for always caring enough to watch out for me. You are most gracious and I owe most of who I am as a teacher to you both.

Gretchen Willaman, thank you for showing me how to love students well, how to relax and find joy in each moment, and for all those countless favors you've given. I look forward to walking many more miles with you, friend!

And finally, to the Original Superkiddos, I say thank you: Bailey, Desirae, Bode, Mason, Chris, Phoenyx, Kolton, Delaney, Kyra, Ella-Mae, Dillon, Jett, Angela, Jeffery, Aaron, Aden, Kylie, Allie, Genesis, Emilie, Wesley, Tyrell, and Caitlyn. Without you there would be no book. Love to you all.

"Make a careful exploration of who you are and the work you've been given, and sink yourself into that. . . . Each of you must take responsibility for doing the creative best you can with your life." (Galatians 6:4–5, The Message).

CHAPTER 1

EXPANDING WRITING CELEBRATIONS

*It is difficult
to get the news from poems,
yet men die miserably every day
for lack
of what is found there.*
—William Carlos Williams

Mason slouched in the corner of the classroom, doing his best to make his man-sized fifth-grade body disappear. We were a few days into a new writing project—nonfiction state videos. Fellow teacher Keith Bollman was anchoring writing workshop with social studies. Earlier in the week, students selected a state, and now they were finding ways to angle their research toward a fascinating topic.

Mason was hunkered in the corner, notebook open, pencil at attention, staring into space. I settled next to him, leaning against the cabinets. "How's it going?" I asked.

Mason shrugged, his eyes droopy at 8:30 a.m.

"Do you want some help?" I pushed a little harder.

"I just need some time to think."

I was tempted to force Mason into making a list of ideas. I wanted him to talk to me about his chosen state. I expected him to do something.

Instead, I nodded. "Okay," I said, standing up, "I'll check back later."

Mason spent the rest of writing workshop in the corner. Other than drawing two tiny doodles in the corner of his notebook page, he didn't move.

Sometimes the things left unsaid are more powerful than ten teaching points put together. I didn't tell Mason to brainstorm and write down some ideas. I didn't tell him to talk to other writers. I didn't tell him to check out the books around the room. I let Mason have some space. Sometimes space, although difficult to give, is best.

Like many of our students, life is hard in Mason's house. Sometimes our students' problems make it hard for us to breathe. The classroom becomes stuffy with the reality of life outside of school. The problems are big.

I think about William Carlos Williams's words that opened this chapter, coming back to them as I think deeply about celebration. I must admit, when I first began teaching I thought celebration was fluff. It was the cherry on top, the bonus day in writing workshop. It wasn't the serious business of writing. Williams compares poetry to news, and then twists the words, making us realize even if poetry isn't "serious business," it is still essential to life.

The next day Mason sat, hunkered in the same spot, intent over the tablet in his lap. I checked in with him again. "What are you working on?" I asked.

"Research," he said.

I looked at the screen on his knees. He was on YouTube, searching videos. "What are you learning?"

Mason tapped the screen, and a video began to play. He turned down the volume. I expected another one-word answer.

"Yesterday, I decided I wanted to learn about airplanes. There's a big aerospace museum in Michigan. They've got a ton of videos on YouTube about the planes."

I nodded, staying silent. Mason continued, "So I'm thinking I'll highlight three planes from the museum for my video. I'm interested in planes and probably other people are too. Can that be my angle?"

"Sounds good. Do you need anything to help you get started?"

Mason shook his head. His notebook was opened to the page with the previous day's tiny doodles, his pencil waiting to put marks on the lines. The tablet was balanced on his knees. "I'm just going to watch these videos today."

Sometimes leaving things unsaid is more difficult than knowing what to say. I wanted to tell him to make a list of possible planes to learn about. I wanted to tell him to set up a notes page in his notebook. I wanted to tell him to look at sites other than YouTube. Instead, I smiled at Mason and said, "I hope you get a lot of ideas from your research today."

Like many of our students, Mason doesn't believe in himself as a writer. For years as an instructional coach, I've watched him try to disappear in writing workshop, making tiny doodles in the corners of pages. The promise of a big hoopla of a party once the writing is finished isn't going to inspire him to write. He's not that kind of kid. He needs more.

During the share session at the end of workshop time, I invited students to share their work as researchers. Mason sat on the edge of the circle, too big to be comfortable on the floor, too compliant to ask to sit in a chair, and too passive to be a part of the group. I noticed his doodles remained the same, but he'd jotted a few words, a list, some notes. He kept his head down.

"Mason," I asked, "do you want to share what you learned through your research today?" He shrugged. I waited. Smiled. Waited. Nudged: "I see you have a list in your notebook."

Mason pushed his thick curly hair out of his eyes and said, "There's a lot of planes at a museum in Michigan, but I thought these three were the most interesting. So I wrote them down."

"What else did you write?" Chandler asked.

Everyone waited for Mason to respond. "You know, just the interesting things about the planes so I don't forget."

"Maybe I'll do that too," Chandler said.

Sometimes we catch a ghost of a smile and know something worthy just happened. I wanted to gush over Mason's chicken scratches on notebook pages. I wanted to give him a high five. I wanted to give him a candy bar. Instead, I treated him like every other writer in the community. He did the work expected of a writer. I chose to respect Mason and agreed with Chandler. "That's a good idea. You know, if you haven't written down a few of the key facts you learned today, would you follow Mason's lead and do it now?"

As it is for many of our students, it is a slow transformation for Mason to accept himself as a writer. He continued to research, collecting snippets and learning about airplanes, for the remainder of the week. He sustained work on this research project longer than on any other because he had sustenance necessary for a writer: We were celebrating, in a quiet but powerful way, as Mason took tiny steps toward a writing life.

Williams's words swirl around my mind:

It is difficult
to get the news from poems,
yet men die miserably every day
for lack
of what is found there.

Perhaps celebration is essential to a writing life.

Publication or Celebration: What's the Difference?

As a new teacher, one of my first steps to transform my instruction into a writing workshop was to encourage students to personalize the writing process. From planning to drafting to revising to editing, we envisioned possibilities and found strategies that worked for different writers in the classroom. I used a mantra I adopted from Lucy Calkins and diligently tried to *teach the writer, not the writing . . .* until it came time for a writing celebration.

Perhaps this is because I had a misconception of writing celebrations. I inherently knew celebration was important. I like to get feedback on my own writing, and I knew young writers would as well. However, in my quest to help students prepare to share their writing projects, perfectly executed writing became more important than the learning. My stomach churns just thinking about the abrupt shift in my focus. I empowered students throughout the entire process, teaching *writers*, and then, in the end, swung the importance back to creating a perfect piece of *writing*. As we neared the end of a project, we began talking about publishing. There is merit in this work, as publication is part of the writing process. However, when it comes to the final piece, we tend to place the emphasis on perfect writing. The writer fades to the background and often stays there when we honor perfect writing instead of growing writers. Today, I've learned to celebrate the writer throughout the process (including publishing) in order to teach writers rather than demand perfection in writing.

Sometimes teachers use the terms *publication* and *celebration* interchangeably. (I know I did!) They are different. Publication is part of the writing process. Celebration is part of the life of a writer. Publication is centered on putting writing into the world. In its most pure form, *publishing* means "to go public." This is definitely something to celebrate! Yet, it is not the only thing to celebrate. Celebration is so much *more*. Celebration ought to wrap around many moments in writing workshop—not just the final product. Celebration is essential to the livelihood of young writers.

My mom is a quilter, and she has taught me to piece blocks and put them together to create a patchwork quilt. One day my writing partner, Mary Helen Gensch, helped me see how the patchwork quilt could help me articulate the difference between publishing and celebrating. The stages of the writing process are like the pieces of fabric. They are significant and important. It's necessary to recognize when students make solid plans, embark on significant revision, and publish lovely products. The writing wouldn't exist without these experiences of the writer. Now think about the stitches. They are woven into the very fiber of the patchwork quilt. They are holding together each piece. They are small but mighty. The quilt would not exist without the stitches. Celebration is the stitches.

Writers, especially the young writers in our classrooms, are on a journey, constantly changing and learning and growing. Celebration embraces this journey. Celebration allows writers to revel in their personal writing processes. It provides time for reflection and growth. After all, this is the point of writing instruction in elementary school. Students are developing their skills as writers. We don't expect perfection. We expect growth. It is critical for the learning and growth to be honored and celebrated—not only during publication but throughout the entire process—so students have the stamina to continue writing day in and day out.

When young writers are encouraged, they are fueled to keep writing. This is the objective of celebration. Celebration nourishes the writer. Writers cannot be sustained on publication alone. It is through celebration that we are able to carry on in the midst of the hard work of writing. In fact, celebration pushes us past the difficult and frustrating parts of writing. When we adopt an attitude of celebration, there are several important messages we send about being a writer.

Celebration Messages

Message 1: The writer is more important than the writing.

By honoring the writer throughout the process, we send the message that growth is the top priority. When displaying perfect pieces of writing, the emphasis is on the product. It is true that writers often write for an audience; however, when we celebrate only after writing is "fancied up," we inadvertently send the message that the product matters more than a student's growth as a writer.

Message 2: Writers celebrate throughout the writing process.

Dig into the background of your favorite writer and you will find their writing life is much deeper than their books on the shelf or their articles in a newspaper or magazine. The products we see are a sliver of the daily grind. If they only celebrated upon publication, their lives would be dreary. Most writers talk about having a group of other people they turn to throughout the process. This group often celebrates the little steps along the way to publication.

Message 3: Learning, growing writers are the goal.

Learning to write well is the goal of writing workshop. Aiming for perfection nearly always gets in the way of learning. Taking risks, playing with craft, and testing conventions are all essential to the growth of a writer. When we celebrate throughout the process, students develop courage to take risks in their writing.

Message 4: Personalizing the writing process is important to writers.

As writers, we can choose how to plan, when to draft, and our approach to revision. We can decide how best to edit our work, and even who reads our writing. We can't, however, select a major publishing house as a publisher or demand that the *New York Times* publish an article. The final stage of the writing process—publication— is not always in the control of the writer. Jane Yolen gives this advice in *Take Joy: A Writer's Guide to Loving the Craft:* "Once you have committed any words to the page and have sent your manuscript off to the publisher, it is mostly beyond your capacity to make anything happen in the publishing of your work" (2006, 10).

Still, the product matters to writers. Ultimately, we are writing *something*. And we want this *something* to be good. We want it to be meaningful, well crafted, and conventionally correct. However, the way to do so is by refining the writing process. By becoming stronger in planning, drafting, revising, and editing, we are able to create stronger products. When we honor the individualized writing processes that lead to products, we stay true to the purpose of celebration.

Message 5: Everyone has a story to share.

There are gobs of writers just waiting to be published, and few will become Pulitzer Prize–winning journalists, Poet Laureates, or *New York Times* best-sellers. The point of learning to be a writer isn't to become famous. The purpose of being a writer is to communicate clearly, to come to new understandings, and to connect to others. If our students are going to grow up to be active citizens in the world, it is important for them to learn at a young age that their words matter. When we celebrate throughout the process, we help students become people who know their words can influence, encourage, and incite change.

Celebration as an Anchor

In June 2010 I started a writing group. I knew that if I wanted to keep writing, I needed a group of writers to hold me accountable. I didn't want to float in the vast ocean of words without others to anchor me.

During our first writing group meeting we huddled around a tiny table in the lobby of a hotel and shared our writing plans. As I listened to the others share, I soon realized it wasn't accountability that I needed, but rather people with whom to celebrate the little moments of being a writer. Unable to contain myself, I declared, "No matter what, we will celebrate the little things." This group wasn't going to be about publication. It was about being a writer—collecting words and stories and ideas and research and putting those things on the page. It wasn't about a product. It was about a way of life.

Celebration became our anchor. In fact, it soon became the only "rule" for our writing group—we would celebrate together. When an idea for a book pricked at the edge of someone's mind, we celebrated. When a member decided to make a list of agents to *maybe, someday, perhaps* contact, we celebrated. When someone finished a chapter or even simply thought about a new angle for their character or tried a new genre, we celebrated. In fact, most of our time is spent in celebration.

Now, our celebrations don't require party hats and cupcakes and those little horns you blow. Celebration, the kind that is the core of a writing life, is much more than fluff, and usually it's a lot quieter. It wraps around our minds, pulling us back to our notebooks in order to live as writers. Celebration nourishes and nudges and makes us stronger writers.

What would happen if celebration, this genuine kind of celebration, was stitched into the very fibers of our writing workshops? How can we help students strengthen their own writing by helping them develop a core that will sustain them to keep working with words even on the hard days?

I've come to realize that three factors make a genuine celebration. First, a writer needs a *response*. Another person reads my writing and then responds with his or her thoughts. The more specific the response, the more it affects me as a writer. The response nudges me to gain insight into my writing and into my writing process. This leads me into *reflection*, a second component of a genuine celebration. It is essential to reflect on my writing and my process in order to develop as a writer. Finally, when the response and reflection come together, I'm able to *rejoice* in my writing life. I find new energy through genuine celebration and am more connected to my writer self.

Writing is worthwhile in and of itself. It's important for students and teachers to internalize this. We don't need to think up gimmicks to convince students to write. The intrinsic reward for writing is enough. In *The Writing Workshop: Working Through the Hard Parts (And They're All Hard Parts)*, Katie Wood Ray tells a story of her teacher education students experiencing writing workshop. At one point, Katie shares, the students talked about writing workshop being a more fun way to teach writing. She writes:

> They are indignant and unable to understand how a teacher could possibly choose not to have a writing workshop when it's so much more fun for students than doing language arts exercises from a textbook. And then I have to do my big blowup: "You think teachers have writing workshops because they're *fun* for students? Is *that* what you think this is about? If that were true we might as well have them all line dancing! Line dancing is *fun!*"
>
> I have to help my students understand that teaching writing in a workshop setting is highly theoretical teaching. That's why we do it—because it's theoretical. Every aspect of the workshop is set up to support children learning to do what writers really do. The teaching is challenging because what writers do is engage in a complex, multilayered, slippery process to produce texts. The writing itself is very satisfying, even fun at times, but that's the *truth* of writing. It's not some motivational game we set up to keep children's interest. If that were all we wanted, we would do things that were far less challenging for us as teachers. (2001, 46)

When our students look back at writing workshop, I hope they remember all that writing gives them and finding their voices and the way their words tugged at another person. I hope they remember reaching new understandings because they put words on the page and the really great feeling that comes from using conventions to make their voices ring clear. I hope they remember more than a cool party.

How Do I Know Celebration Is Essential?

Writing has always come easily to me. And then things changed in July 2010. My friend, twenty-year-old Nate Cain, died unexpectedly. I got the call about the time I was expecting him for dinner, pulling one of his favorite side dishes, cheesy potatoes, out of the oven. My husband and I went to the hospital. We stood beside his body. We gave his eulogy.

When we came home after the funeral dinner, I sat in Nate's spot on our couch, emotionally drained, and felt compelled to write. I was surprised to find a young adult novel begin to emerge. I didn't write fiction. I didn't write for teens. I didn't know what to do as this kind of writer. But I didn't have a choice. I had to write the story.

I got a good dose of what students experience in writing workshop, having to write all kinds of things they've never written before, having no idea how or why they should keep going. I often felt lost in the process, feeling inadequate as a writer. I wondered if I was wasting my time and if maybe I should clean the house instead.

My writing group said, "Keep going." My critique partner, Ruth Metcalfe, gave specific response to my drafts. Even when the writing was less than perfect . . . even when the story was hanging together by threads . . . even when I had to revise the beginning for the forty-eighth time, she continued to give specific response. She pushed me to reflect on the story as well as on my process. She asked questions, giving me guidance and helping me reach new understandings. And she didn't forget the sustenance I needed most, a little bit of rejoicing. She'd highlight a line and comment, "I hope you're proud of this line." She'd talk me through a draft, telling me the parts that stayed with her as a reader. All these things were a celebration of my work as a writer.

Ruth showed me what it means to have a genuine celebration, one that honors the writer and lifts the writing to a new level. I wasn't writing my YA fiction story for publication. But the writing was still important. I couldn't have finished if it weren't for the one rule of our writing group: *We will celebrate.*

By celebrating the small accomplishments as writers, big growth can happen. Altering the purpose of celebration starts small when we shift to genuine celebration through responding, reflecting, and rejoicing in the writing community. Chapter 2 breaks down these essentials and offers a rationale and specific ideas to make these essentials part of your writing community. Chapter 3 takes a look at how to use technology to continue the celebration online. Chapter 4 digs into the behind-the-scenes thinking of celebrating publication while maintaining a focus on the writer. Finally, Chapter 5 offers a slew of writer-centered end-of-the-unit ideas for when you want to host a celebration with your writers *and* the writing they've produced.

It's time to expand the idea of celebration to include the *process* writers go through *and* the products they create. Let's build an approach that stitches celebration into the heart of all writers. Be ready to learn to refuel the writers in your classroom, even on the tough days.

CHAPTER 2

THE BACKBONE OF ALL CELEBRATIONS

*Everything is held together by stories. That is all that is
holding us together, stories and compassion.*
—Barry Lopez

Dillon was a twin, the youngest of four brothers with parents who
worked as hard as possible to keep their family afloat. He often came
to school hungry and tired. Writing wasn't at the top of his list of
things to do each day. Dillon was a gentle, mild-mannered kid who
had absolutely no confidence in his writing. Not only that, he had
no desire to write. He hid under tables during writing time, avoided
talking during sharing time, and never completed a writing project
for the first several months of school. It was obvious that he believed
his stories weren't important to anyone . . . not even to himself.

We talked with Dillon a lot about how his stories were unique
and how no one else could tell his stories for him. We gave him extra
time to write and we gave him special mentor texts to use, and still
nothing seemed to really fuel him to write.

Finally he wrote a two-page spread about himself sneaking onto
an airplane to New York. We were a little surprised to find he'd suddenly decided to write. We noticed this was some of his best work
ever. Yes, it was only two pages. No, it didn't tell an entire story.

But it was a start. He gave us an inch; we needed to go the mile to give him the needed confidence to continue. This might be the only chance we had. Genuine celebration was our best option.

We color-scanned Dillon's spread onto our classroom blog and allowed the other students to comment on Dillon's work during a lesson. We discussed the illustration technique Dillon used and how it might work for others. Students responded in authentic ways and then went off to work.

We kept a close eye on Dillon, almost holding our breath wondering if this book would be banned to the "Not Finished" pile in his folder. The days unfolded and Dillon continued to work on his story, finally writing the final scene. We celebrated with Dillon on the day he finished his book. He offered a proud smile and mumbled, "I'm going to start another." He'd gained the confidence he needed to create and write his own stories.

Every person has a story worth telling. These stories are worthy because they foster connections, creating empathy for others, and give us a stronger understanding of ourselves. It is important that we consider our stories, opinions, and interests worthy of becoming words on the page. Not because of publication, but for something bigger. The mission of writing workshop is to help people learn to be writers for life. Genuine celebration aids in this mission.

Celebration isn't about writing for publication; it's about writing for meaning. Expanding our view of celebrations is not necessarily about changing the way we are currently celebrating. There are remarkable writing celebrations in classrooms across the globe. Film festivals, poetry jams, and writing cafés are powerful means of celebrating. Changing our view of celebration doesn't mean scrapping the celebrations already in place. It's about expanding the scope of writing celebrations to consider *what* we celebrate and *when* we celebrate. Instead of celebrating only products, let's celebrate process too. Instead of celebrating only at the end of a unit, let's celebrate throughout it too.

If we waited to celebrate until after Dillon finished a writing project, we would still be waiting. Because we expanded our view of celebration and decided it didn't have to happen only at the end of the project, Dillon was nourished as a writer. Dillon realized how much his story mattered because he received responses and was nudged to reflect as a writer. Soon we were celebrating Dillon's stories—both in process and completion.

It started with valuing the glimmer of the writer we were seeing in Dillon. Then we provided an opportunity for *response*. Students responded and it fueled Dillon, causing him to *reflect* on his writing life and keep going. As a community we *rejoiced*.

Response, reflection, and rejoicing position us to celebrate the writer in addition to the writing. These frames also allow us to celebrate throughout the writing process instead of solely at the end. They move us to a focus on learning as writers. Our celebrations nourish writers, nudging them to continue writing with expertise and energy.

Learning to Respond

Response is noticing and naming the things a writer is doing and then sharing how we are affected as readers. This kind of response doesn't come automatically, but it can be studied, practiced, and refined. Students must learn how to respond to other writers in a respectful and useful manner. In the push to align with Common Core Standards, learning to give valuable responses is no longer an option. More importantly, if we are going to create classrooms with a core of celebration, feedback becomes essential. If students are going to learn to give powerful feedback, we must create structures and intentional learning opportunities for them to become the kinds of people who offer support and encouragement.

It begins with students receiving response to their own writing. Students experience the power of response as teachers give specific feedback during conferences. Conferring is an essential part of writing workshop, so it comes as no surprise that a conference is the best place to model constructive feedback.

If we explicitly teach the format of a conference, then students become aware of the way feedback sounds. In primary classrooms, I often use a chart (Figure 2.1) to outline the structure of a conference.

As students gain experience in writing workshop, they come to expect the predictable format of a conference. When our conferences include both compliments and teaching points, students learn that feedback encourages *and* nudges us as writers.

Figure 2.1 This chart helps young writers internalize the predictable nature of a conversation during a conference.

Author and educator Carl Anderson often encourages us to discuss different conference roles with intermediate-grade students. Recently I used this idea to create a chart to share with fourth graders (Figure 2.2). As students gain a deeper understanding of the things to talk about as writers and responders they will be able to offer more thoughtful and effective feedback.

Charts create visual reminders for how to talk as writers and responders. We have a natural tendency to avoid hurting other people, so response becomes a tricky terrain to navigate. There is a wide chasm around encouragement and constructive response. We can fall off the cliff with safe generalities, lavish praise, and rude criticism. It takes a lot of practice to tailor our responses to become both encouraging and constructive. I've learned how to do this through responding to thousands of student and adult writers.

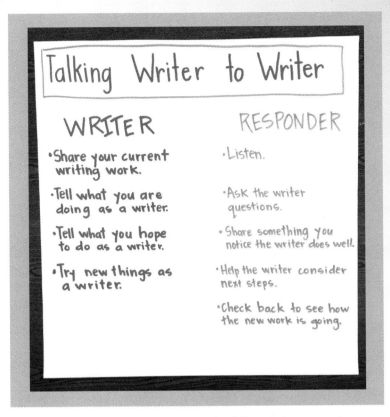

Figure 2.2 Intermediate writers can consider different roles in a conference to grow into more effective peer responders.

Every March (and every Tuesday during the other eleven months of the year) Stacey Shubitz and I have hosted a writing challenge on the blog I cofounded, *Two Writing Teachers*. The Slice of Life challenge is twofold: (1) to write a slice-of-life story every day for the month and (2) to comment on other writers' slices. We first established this challenge to help teachers relate to their student writers, who have to write daily in writing workshop. We knew the challenge would help teachers develop a writing habit. What surprised me was how much Slice of Life has helped me learn to give powerful feedback.

As a writer, I've realized how much feedback matters to me. I love (and I mean *lovelovelove*) to get comments on my blog posts. As I've read the feedback to my writing, I've learned what is important for me to hear. I've learned what inspires and what nudges. I've even learned what I don't need to hear and what doesn't hurt, but doesn't help either.

All that I've learned can be boiled down to this: *Specificity matters*. When someone comments with, "I love this!" it doesn't mean as much as specific feedback. However, I was encouraged and nudged as a writer when Alan Wright left this comment:

> *Trust grows slowly. It requires patience. The honesty of this piece requires trust from your readers—and empathy. When we empower others, we empower ourselves. More power to you for sharing this raw and revealing piece, Ruth. I feel privileged.*

From Alan I was *inspired* to write more about the hard parts of adopting older children. From Alan, I *learned* to trust my readers and that it's worth the risk to write with raw emotion.

Receiving feedback is only part of the process of learning to construct powerful responses. It is also by *giving* feedback that we learn how to talk to writers in meaningful ways. As part of the Slice of Life challenge I comment on as many slicers as possible. This process has forced me to learn to give meaningful response quickly.

Because of the Slice of Life challenge, I've become more efficient in my conferring. I can pinpoint specific choices people have made as writers and mold what I notice into compliments. This kind of feedback is a celebration of the writer and crucial to growth. The way we hone this skill is to spend time offering response to others.

Feedback is the key to creating a community of writers who celebrate together. Modeling feedback for students through our conferring is essential, but it is only the first step in the process. Through direct instruction, partnerships, and, eventually, writing groups, students will also hone their skills in giving and receiving meaningful responses.

Response in Action

The mini-lesson is the structure in writing workshop designed to deliver direct instruction in order for students to become stronger writers. We commonly give instruction in craft and conventions during mini-lessons. Mini-lessons about honing the writing process are also important. When we teach students how to respond to writers we often unlock celebration. Celebration comes alive and nourishes the hearts of writers as students learn to respond in ways that encourage and nudge others.

What kinds of mini-lessons can we teach to help student writers learn how to give powerful responses to other writers? This is the question I asked as I started to support teachers in establishing writing partnerships and groups in their classrooms. In order to answer this question, I depended on my own writing group experience. I also observed students working in partnerships and noticed what they did well and how they could become more efficient. Through mini-lessons students will learn specific strategies for giving meaningful feedback; however most of the learning will happen through the process of actually giving authentic responses. Like many other new situations, giving feedback can feel awkward at first. We can make it easier by establishing writing partnerships. A writing partnership is a pair of students who meet together regularly over time. Partnerships allow students to get to know one other writer's work. Over time, the partnerships become more comfortable, which positions students to move beyond generalities such as "It's good" or "I like your story" and into the realm of encouraging and nudging each other as writers.

Your group of students as well as your own preferences will influence the way you decide to establish partnerships. The good news is, there isn't a "wrong" way to establish partnerships (other than not establishing them!). Although an option, I tend not to give students a free-for-all choice when deciding on their writing partners. But in upper grades, it is wise to gather some student input for writing partners. Sometimes there are underlying factors making writing partnerships fail that have nothing to do with writing and everything to do with social experiences. As teachers we don't always know all of the conflicts and barriers between students that may lead to ineffective partnerships. Therefore, I ask students in upper grades to complete the writing partnership survey shown in Figure 2.3. (Note: All figures with a web icon next to them are available as downloads on this book's companion website, www.stenhouse.com/celebratingwriters.)

Name_____

WRITING PARTNERSHIP SURVEY

Writers depend on others to encourage them to keep writing and to nudge them to grow.

Throughout the year we will depend on one another to encourage and nudge us. In fact, you will get to know one person's writing really well because you will be **WRITING PARTNERS** for the rest of the year. Eventually we will form **WRITING GROUPS** by matching two writing partnerships to form a group.

Long story short: You will meet with your WRITING PARTNER for the entire year. In order to help form successful partnerships, please complete the following survey. Don't forget to be kind with your words.

- -

How do you feel about yourself as a writer?

_____

_____

Is there someone in the class who makes you feel good about yourself? If so, please write their name and tell how they make you feel good about yourself.

_____

_____

You are the kind of person who can work with almost anyone; however, is there someone you would find it very difficult to have as a writing partner this school year? If so, please write their name and tell why it would be difficult to work together.

_____

_____

Figure 2.3 Older students can help determine writing partnerships by completing this survey or one similar to it.

No matter the age of students, I tend to look at confidence as a determining factor in creating writing partnerships. Since encouragement and nudges are crucial to meaningful feedback, I've noticed that students who are confident are often natural at nudging others to grow. Students who are timid tend to be gentle encouragers. By creating a partnership with a student who is apt to encourage and a student who is apt to nudge, we've established a pair who can learn from one another.

In addition, especially for our youngest writers, I find it important to arrange partnerships so there is at least one student who is willing to begin a conversation. When two primary nontalkers get together, they will be dependent on you, the teacher, to model conversation for them. Since it is important for you to observe all partnerships, it is best to avoid this issue when arranging partnerships.

For the most part, I tend not to let writing experience levels determine partnerships. Often the most inexperienced writers in the room give the most meaningful feedback, whereas the strongest writers in the room sometimes need support in developing strategies to give effective responses. However, I have spent time with teachers looking over local assessment data, such as NWEA, in order to get a more well-rounded view of the writers in the classroom. Sometimes these data influence our decisions when establishing writing partnerships.

There isn't a science to forming partnerships. There isn't a foolproof plan. Instead, plan to roll up your sleeves, look at a variety of information you have about your students, and ultimately depend on your gut to make a list of writing partners.

Once partnerships are established, plan to observe and rearrange as needed in order to position every student for a successful writing partnership experience. Be honest with students; let them know there is a trial period for writing partners and that there may be some changes in the first few weeks. For upper grades, you may want to check in with your students to gain valuable insight in the productivity of the partnerships. Figure 2.4 shows a possible reflection sheet students can use to consider the effectiveness of their partnerships and you can use to determine whether partnerships are valuable.

I ask students to sit next to their writing partners during the mini-lessons. This way, students talk with their partners almost daily during the mini-lessons, and I am able to listen in on the conversations. This practice also helps streamline the mini-lessons, because students are used to talking with the same person. Additionally, students don't have to spend time recapping their latest writing projects, because their partners already know. Students can focus their discussions on the teaching points of the mini-lessons rather than on summarizing their writing.

Name _____ Writing Partner _____ Date: _____

Writing Partnership Check-In

What do you like about meeting with your writing partner?

_____

_____

How does your writing partner encourage and nudge you as a writer?

_____

_____

What changes do you and your writing partner need to make in order to be more efficient when meeting together?

_____

_____

Figure 2.4 Older students can reflect on their writing partnerships to help you determine whether they are effective.

About once a week, plan to designate a share session for writing partnership meetings. This allows time for students to talk in-depth about their writing work. Initially, it is important to scaffold partners' discussions to help them encourage and nudge each other. Feedback stems, as shown in Figure 2.5, are one way to help anchor conversations. These conversation starters help students shore up their responses to one another, moving the feedback from "That's good" to something meaningful. This empowers the writer to continue writing and to become stronger.

As you walk around the room during the writing partnership share session, you should notice that the energy level among writers is high. Genuine celebration will wrap itself around the partnerships, giving the needed energy and courage for writers to keep going.

As students engage in partnerships, they have the opportunity to give and receive response in a safe relationship. Once partnerships are strong and meaningful feedback becomes the norm, then it's time to establish writing groups.

Like partnerships, writing groups allow members to build relationships and become comfortable with one another in order to provide powerful responses. Writing groups of three to five members become miniature writing communities within the classroom. The responses become varied, and the group learns to value the different strengths of each member.

To form writing groups, combine two sets of partnerships. (Sometimes writing groups have three to five members because there are an uneven number of students in your class.) When creating writing groups, I tend to start by ranking partnerships from most effective to least effective. Then I pair partnerships from the top of the list with those at the bottom.

There are a few ways I determine whether a writing partnership is effective. First, effective writing partnerships are joyful. The students in them offer both encouragement and nudges to each other. They have also moved from being dependent on the feedback stems to bringing unique questions and needs to their meetings. The effective partnership will serve as a model for the other partners.

Try these starters to offer valuable feedback to other writers.

See Online

I liked this part because . . .

I didn't understand because . . .

I wish I could have known more about . . .

I want to write like you and try . . .

You made me think . . .

Keep writing because . . .

Figure 2.5 Students can use these conversation starters to help give meaningful feedback to one another.

From Process
to Product

Writing groups allow students to celebrate their writing lives regularly throughout the school year instead of celebrating only the products every few months. However, when end-of-unit celebrations do occur, students are able to give solid responses to other members of the class because they have practiced with their partners and writing groups. The responses are rich and students are able to see how their work throughout the writing process leads to a product that impacts others. In the end-of-unit celebrations, the celebration that has strengthened writers' cores day in and day out is unleashed to wrap around the products they create as well.

Kinds of Responses

There are basically three kinds of responses:

1. Oral
2. Written
3. Digital

Response is an integral component in moving more formal, end-of-unit writing celebrations into experiences that focus on the writer. As part of formal celebrations, older students can record their responses on a comment sheet like the one in Figure 2.6. This allows each writer to have a record of the way their writing is affecting others. Written response also gives more people the opportunity to share how the writing is affecting them. If students read to themselves during the formal celebration, everyone can give and receive comments at the same time. If students read their work aloud, the audience can write their responses on sticky notes and then put them on a single comment sheet for the writer. Both of these strategies allow several writers to receive several responses.

Figure 2.6 During a celebration, each student has one of these pages for other students to comment on his or her work. These often become precious tokens of encouragement to writers.

Younger students can receive a written record of the responses to their writing during a formal celebration if an adult records verbal responses. This record is a nice document to send home with a student's writing so parents can see the way we are encouraging and inspiring writers at school. In the sample response sheet shown in Figure 2.7, there is space for an adult to record the response and a space for the students who give the feedback to write their names.

Another way to add significance to oral response is to ask students to share with the whole class the responses that were most beneficial to them. When the writer shares a meaningful response with the whole group, it gives weight to the response and makes it more memorable. It also gives the entire class an opportunity to hear meaningful responses and then refine their own responses to make them more useful. Ultimately, though, it places the emphasis back on the writer as opposed to the product. This is the power of response —it accentuates the writer, making formal celebrations reflect the pure heart of writing workshop.

Digital responses can come in the form of comments to student work posted on a blog or comments on other social networks, such as Twitter or a classroom Facebook page. As we prepare students for twenty-first-century literacy skills, collaborating via technology is key. Social networks make it possible to communicate with family and friends near and far as well as with others around the globe. When we engage with one another in these virtual spaces, we offer more opportunities for celebrating the writers in our classrooms. We'll explore this idea further in Chapter 3.

Today We Celebrated as Writers!

_____said about my writing . . .

_____said about my writing . . .

_____said about my writing . . .

_____said about my writing . . .

Special people from around the school joined us today for writing workshop. We shared our books in small groups and then told the writers things we liked. The guests recorded the responses for us to keep. We can't wait to share our books with our families and friends!

Figure 2.7 Using this response sheet, adults can help students remember what was said about their writing by recording it for them.

Learning to Reflect

Common Core Standards of College and Career Readiness Anchor Standards for Writing demand students "develop and strengthen writing as needed by planning, revising, editing, rewriting, or trying a new approach"(NGA/CCSSO 2010). One of the only ways to know if students are trying a new approach is through reflection. Reflection is thinking about what you do and how you feel about it. The heart of reflective practice is using self-evaluation to strengthen your craft. As writers, we can reflect either on process or product. As we reflect on our own writing process, we learn how to work more efficiently as writers. It is important to note that through reflection, we realize that process changes according to genre, topic, audience, and purpose.

Personally, my writing process is streamlined, succinct, and fast when it comes to writing blog posts. However, when I work on poetry, it is more circular, and I come back to the words again and again, reworking them alone and aloud. My process changes again when I tackle a larger project. I tend to plan more extensively, and talk becomes crucial to my success as a writer. I find these insights into my writing process valuable. We should help students find valuable insights like these as well.

One way to encourage reflection is to weave it into the conversations of partnerships and writing groups. By asking students either to open or close their conversations with statements about how their writing is going and why they feel this way, we nudge them into reflective practice. Conversations with my writing group always include reflective practice. They have to in order for me to continue growing as a writer. If I don't reflect on my process, if I don't reflect on my craft, then it is impossible for me to grow. I believe the same is true for young writers. Without reflection, they are missing out on an opportunity to grow.

Much of the reflective conversation within partnerships and writing groups is centered on the writer's process. It is important to identify what works well for us as writers and how we can create situations in order to be most productive. However, there is also a time when we reflect on the writing itself. This may happen during partnerships or writing groups or it may happen during end-of-unit celebrations. In order to hold true to genuine celebration, we should focus on the meaning of the writing. How do structure, craft, and conventions help (or hinder) the meaning to unfold for the reader? Through reflecting on the product, we often gain insight into things we should do as writers to improve the writing process.

Kinds of Reflections

Reflections can be personal, public, or digital. The kind of reflection we use is dependent on the purpose. Personal reflections are for the writer's eyes only and are designed to stretch the writer, encouraging risks in process or product. A public reflection is intended to be shared with the larger writing community, with the purpose of inspiring others to take risks as writers. Finally, a digital reflection allows for sharing with even more people and provides another opportunity to inspire and encourage.

Personal Reflections

Personal reflections can be written in writers' notebooks or in margins of drafts. When writers notice something about themselves, they can jot it down. In order to develop as writers, we can take time to jot a writer's notebook entry considering what we do well as writers and what we would like to learn to do. Another option is to make a list or a T-chart identifying our strengths and hopes as writers. Two of my own notebook entries in which I reflect on my writing life are shown in Figures 2.8 and 2.9. Figure 2.8 is a response to the Write Fifteen Minutes a Day challenge hosted each August by Laurie Halse Anderson on her blog (madwomanintheforest.com/blog). She challenged us to list our strengths and weaknesses as a fiction writer. In Figure 2.9, I reflected on my history as a writer. Reflection is an integral part of my writing life. It helps me see growth, it inspires me to continue writing, and it forces me to believe in myself. When we complete these kinds of reflections for ourselves, we can share them with students to empower them to dig deep and consider the work they are doing as writers.

In addition to completing personal reflections in my writer's notebook, I encounter personal reflection when I meet with my critique partner or writing group. A conversation about our writing processes often bolsters us and provides renewed energy for a writing project. We can encourage young writers to engage in this kind of reflection by having them use a partnership share session to discuss their writing processes. This same format can be used for students to reflect on their products. "What is going well?" and "What could be changed?" are great springboards for a reflective conversation.

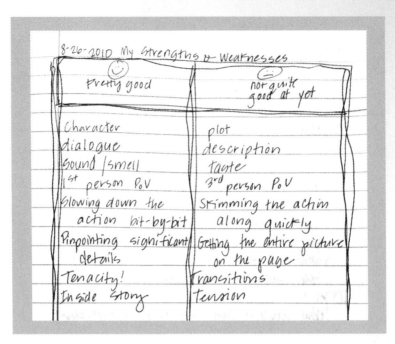

8-26-2010 My Strengths & Weaknesses

☺ Pretty good	☺ not quite good at yet
Character	plot
dialogue	description
sound/smell	taste
1st person PoV	3rd person PoV
slowing down the action bit-by-bit	skimming the action along quickly
Pinpointing significant details	Getting the entire picture on the page
Tenacity!	Transitions
Inside Story	Tension

Figure 2.8 Reflections on my strengths and needs as a writer in response to a challenge by Laurie Halse Anderson

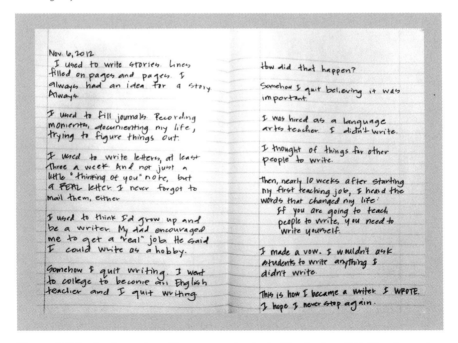

Nov. 6, 2012

I used to write stories. Lines filled on pages and pages. I always had an idea for a story. Always.

I used to fill journals. Recording moments, documenting my life, trying to figure things out.

I used to write letters, at least three a week. And not just a little "thinking of you" note, but a REAL letter I never forgot to mail them, either.

I used to think I'd grow up and be a writer. My dad encouraged me to get a "real" job. He said I could write as a hobby.

Somehow I quit writing. I went to college to become an English teacher and I quit writing.

How did that happen?

Somehow I quit believing it was important.

I was hired as a language arts teacher. I didn't write.

I thought of things for other people to write.

Then, nearly 10 weeks after starting my first teaching job, I heard the words that changed my life:
If you are going to teach people to write, you need to write yourself.

I made a vow. I wouldn't ask students to write anything I didn't write.

This is how I became a writer. I WROTE. I hope I never stop again.

Figure 2.9 A reflection on how I became a writer by looking back and thinking forward

From time to time, students complete a formal reflection. This is designed to help students gain more insight into themselves as writers as well as to give me an understanding of their writing processes. Much of what we do as writers is an unseen process; in order to know whether students have an effective writing process, a more formal reflection is necessary.

Although the purpose remains the same, formal reflections can be angled for the experiences of your group of student writers. Figures 2.10 and 2.11 show two examples of formal reflection forms, each geared for a different experience level.

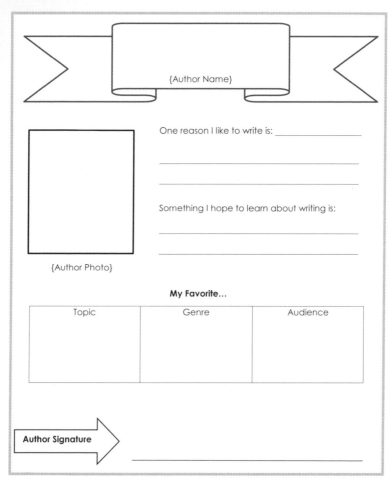

Figure 2.10 This formal reflection sheet works well for students who are new to writing workshop. They write their names—big and fancy—in the box at the top. Then they can either paste or draw an author photo of themselves in the frame. This can also be used as a basis for a "Meet the Authors" bulletin board.

Writing Reflection

Author: _____ **Date:** _____

Title of Writing Project: _____

How did you plan?

_____

_____

Was drafting easy or difficult? _____

List the strategies you used to revise:

    ✓ _____

    ✓ _____

What can you (as the writer) do to help your writing partnership?

_____

_____

How did you edit?

_____

_____

What do you like best about your writing?

_____

_____

What was the hardest part of this writing project?

_____

_____

Figure 2.11 This formal reflection sheet is appropriate for students experienced with writing workshop. By completing an author profile, students reflect on their writing lives.

Public Reflections

Reflections that are shared with an audience are helpful for writers as well. One way students can go public is by interviewing one another. When answering questions about their writing lives, students enter into reflective practice. In order to help students prepare for interviews, consider snagging a colleague and modeling an interview in front of the class. Your students will enjoy getting to know you as a writer and they will see, firsthand, the format of an interview. Next, brainstorm with students possible questions that would help writers talk about their writing lives. Figure 2.12 shares a few possibilities you might generate with your class.

By giving partners a chance to share their answers privately between themselves first, they often will feel more comfortable sharing their reflections with the whole class during an end-of-workshop share session. Sharing in this way is powerful because it encourages students to reflect as well as talk like writers. To facilitate the whole-class share, establish a structure within which students will feel more comfortable. One possible structure is a talk show format. Set up two chairs, a makeshift microphone or two, and students will be ready to share their interviews publically.

Possible Interview Questions to Help Writers Reflect

Where is your favorite place to write?

What is your favorite writing tool?

What topic do you love to write about?

What do you do when you get stuck as a writer?

What is your favorite thing about writing?

What makes it difficult to write?

What is the next thing you are planning to write?

Figure 2.12 Possible Interview Questions to Help Writers Reflect

I once met a teacher who used a large refrigerator box and cut a window in it, then painted on the edges to make it look like a television. Students sat inside the box and performed their interviews during the share session. What a great way to empower reflective practice.

Digital Reflections

Digital formats provide another forum for reflection. I appreciate digital reflections, because a larger community confirms and challenges my thinking about my life as a writer. Often I blog about my writing process or my current writing project, which gives me the opportunity to think critically about my writing life as well as the chance to get feedback from other writers.

As I write this, I'm monitoring a blog post I wrote this morning about writing this book. Throughout the day I've returned to the post to find encouragement and fuel to continue working. I've also updated my status on this project as the day goes on. It holds me accountable to keep working (and hopefully meet the deadline). The nature of a blog provides a large community to nudge me as a writer. The reflective nature of my writing blog, *Ruth Ayres Writes*, has strengthened my writing life more than any other choice I've made as a writer. It provides a place for me to house my reflections as well as a forum for others to encourage, inspire, and nudge me as a writer. Reflection is powerful, and it is important to help students develop this aspect of their writing lives.

Rejoicing

Bigger than cupcakes and punch, rejoicing is about infusing joy in the daily grind of writing workshop. We do this by celebrating the small steps of being writers. High fives and smiles go far in bringing encouragement to writing workshop. Sometimes rejoicing is quiet. It's a nod of encouragement. It's the space to *not write* on some days, because the words aren't there. It's the pat on the shoulder and a wink across the room when we see students are doing their best as writers. Rejoicing is gracefully affirming every writer in the community and then acknowledging their work as writers.

Rejoicing is also about celebrating the big accomplishments we achieve as writers. By asking students to share a favorite comment about their writing, we rejoice in the good stuff we do as writers. An author's chair provides an opportunity for students to share work they are proud of and gives the community a chance to rejoice with them. We can also put student books in the classroom library, giving members of the class a chance to linger over one another's writing. Go all out and create a label for your book bin; making it stand out will beckon everyone to pull a book from this special basket. Need an idea for a special label? Check out Figures 2.13 and 2.14.

We often rejoice by sharing student work in blog posts and on Twitter or Facebook. These forums allow a bigger audience to rejoice

Figure 2.13 A Sample Label for a Bin of Student Books

Figure 2.14 A Sample Label for a Bin of Student Books

alongside us. Often readers respond with encouragement that fuels writers for the next day's work. Rejoicing during the process as well as rejoicing about finished products is an important part of celebrating the writer's life.

Response + Reflection + Rejoicing = ENERGY

When response, reflection, and rejoicing come together, writers feel a renewed energy for their work. In order to tap this energy as often as possible, it's important to celebrate both the process and the products in writing workshop. This energy is fundamental to the life of a writer. Genuine celebration requires expanding our current thinking of traditional writing celebrations in order to respond, reflect, and rejoice more often about more facets of the writing life.

CHAPTER 3

EXPANDING
CELEBRATIONS ONLINE

*Social media is not a media. The key is to listen, engage,
and build relationships.*

—David Alston

On my last birthday I received more than a hundred electronic birthday wishes via Facebook, Twitter, Blogger, e-mail, and text messages.
It made me realize the influence of social networks in celebrating
the good stuff in life. Our writing lives deserve to be celebrated, and
social networks are a valid place to turn to when considering writing
celebrations.

Celebrating with an online community gives our words the potential to reach people we are unable to connect with in any other
way. Online celebrations provide the opportunity to connect in ways
that mirror the world outside of school. When we Skype with people
in other countries, post writing to a blog, and have a book party on
Twitter, we help students understand the world is connected. No
matter what paths students' lives take, they will live more fulfilling
lives by being globally connected.

Online spaces make the globe smaller. Classrooms become
connected. Suddenly our students are learning the science behind

why we have to talk with our Ireland "Tweeps" in the morning, because they are getting ready to leave school for the afternoon. They are learning new vocabulary from their friends in Australia and Canada. They are talking about snow with students in Africa. Even more important, they are learning how much the kids in these other places are like them. They realize they are learning the same things. They share their stories with one another and realize their feelings transcend continents. A child can sit in my rural Midwest classroom, never leaving the state, and connect with people across the globe.

Through online spaces, students also have a degree of access to authors that before was impossible. If we have a question for an author, we can tweet them, or check their blog for reflections on their writing lives, or follow them on Facebook. Authors are more accessible than ever before. This gives us an opportunity to use them for mentors when it comes to the writing process, not just the final products.

One year I helped lead an author study of Mo Willems in Deborah Nelson's kindergarten classroom. Throughout the unit, I collected video clips of students working and wrote down snippets of their thoughts about writing as they gleaned them from studying Mo Willems. As a final celebration, I arranged the clips together in a video that documented our learning. We shared a link to our YouTube video via Mo Willems's Twitter username, @The_Pigeon. As we tweeted from the interactive whiteboard, students giggled and giggled at the prospect of Mo seeing their video. Within an hour @The_Pigeon retweeted our video celebration. The class cheered, ecstatic that Mo had "joined" their writing celebration.

Not only did Mo join our celebration, but so did parents, grandparents, relatives, and friends. Since the video is on YouTube, people from around the globe were able to celebrate with us. You can celebrate with us too; just take a look at the note that we sent home to families (Figure 3.1). (If you have a smartphone or tablet, you'll be able to scan the QR code and go directly to the video.)

Celebrate with Us!

We will be celebrating our work as writers next Friday at 2:00 pm.
Plan on joining us for a video highlighting our learning. Then there will be time to
read the books we wrote and Mo's books. Younger siblings welcome!

If you are unable to attend, please check out our video on YouTube. You can scan the QR Code
below or find our video on YouTube by searching "Ruth Ayres + Inspired by Mo Willems."

Figure 3.1 The note we sent to families inviting them to celebrate in our classrooms

Learning to Function in Online Social Networks

The children in our classrooms are going to grow up to be part of online social networks. It is inevitable. They are the digital natives of our society. The problem is, they are often self-taught. They know how to use social media, but they haven't thought through how to do so with integrity or effectiveness. The potential hazards this generation of self-taught digital natives might encounter is frightening.

You don't have to look far to find reports of digital tools going awry. Cyber-bullying, harassment, and identity theft top the list. Teens join social networking sites with the encouragement of their friends, but with little information. Who is preparing them to be responsible with their words in these settings?

As elementary teachers, we have the opportunity to model and discuss powerful and responsible ways to use our voices online. When we lead our classrooms into social networks, students see firsthand the appropriate ways to function in these spaces. We can be models for our students and then scaffold them as they enter these worlds alongside us. When we intentionally teach the culture and customs of social networking, students are more prepared to act responsibly when joining social networks on their own.

Teaching students social networking responsibility isn't something that we can afford to postpone. Children are entering social networks at very young ages. Unfortunately, they often aren't taught how to function in these spaces. By beginning to learn the norms of social media in kindergarten, students have more time to observe teachers modeling appropriate use, practice with adult support, and internalize the norms and expectations of an online community. One of the best places to learn the nuances of social media is in school, but it is only possible if teachers establish an online presence as a classroom. Once our presence is established, it becomes a rich forum for celebrating writers.

In order to teach the norms of social networks, we must have candid conversations with our students. These unfold when we are diligent about being considerate and responsible in online spaces. Christi posted a story writen by one of her students about a sleepover of three friends on her classroom blog. Page after page was about two of the boys teasing the third boy. All three boys were in the class and were good friends. Christi thought the story was written in good nature; however, when she shared it online with the class, she noticed the boy who was teased in the story was bothered as she read the book to the class.

Later Christi asked him how he felt about the book. He shrugged his shoulders, saying, "That's just how Brad is. He was teasing."

"Do you want us to take it down?" she asked. He responded with another shrug. Christi explained that the blog was an extension of the classroom. If something was posted that hurt someone, then they would take it down. She explained that it was important to think about how the things we post impact others.

The boy nodded. "Yeah, I think we should take it off then." Within minutes the post was removed. Christi followed up with a conversation with the writer. It's important that students understand the way their words can impact others—both people they know and those they've never met.

These conversations with our young writers are fundamental. Through these conversations, students internalize the importance of being considerate of others' feelings, even in online spaces. In fact, we must be even more deliberate in thinking of others in social networks than in face-to-face interactions, because body language and eye contact are nonexistent online. If we aren't using digital tools alongside our students, then these conversations won't happen. Many times when using Twitter our students have wanted to tell jokes or be silly with students living in other countries. We say, "Yes, that is very funny here, but remember, our friends in Mr. Quinn's class can't see our faces all the way from Ireland, so they might not know we're joking. Is there a better way to say something funny?" This kind of thought-provoking question was always enough to change what our students wanted to post.

Online Spaces to Expand Writing Celebrations

There are a slew of online networks. They come and go. New ones constantly join the scene. It's easy to feel overwhelmed by social media. Where do we begin? Figure 3.2 outlines six online spaces that have the potential to help you expand your writing celebrations. The first four also help students learn the nuances of being a contributing member to social media.

Social Media	Purpose	Technology Needs	Level of Commitment
Blog	Document learning Share writing Respond to writers Reflect as writers Rejoice as writers	Internet access Blog account Scanner or camera	Predictable, regular posts
Twitter	Document learning Share links to blog posts Gather primary research Reflect as writers Rejoice as writers	Internet access Twitter account Student access to computer(s) in order to read and respond to Tweets	Daily
Facebook	Communicate with families Share links to blog posts	Internet access Facebook account Facebook page	Predictable, regular posts
Skype	Communicate with others (classrooms or authors) Respond to writers Reflect as writers Rejoice as writers	Internet access Skype account Camera	One time
YouTube	Share videos Watch videos	Internet access YouTube account (can be linked to Google account)	One time
Pinterest	Gather ideas for writing celebrations Find ways to respond, reflect, and rejoice as writers	Internet access Pinterest account	Teacher use

Figure 3.2 An Overview of Potential Online Spaces to Generate Global Writing Celebrations

Blogs

In my opinion, blogs are one of the best ways to extend writing celebrations online. A classroom blog does take time to establish and update, but it is well worth the effort. Blogs allow people to post as little or as much information as needed with photos, images, videos, and words. Classroom blogs can be fancy or simple, but they all have a common purpose: to give students an audience for their writing and an outlet for their voices. Blogging empowers students to use their voices and share their stories, opinions, and interests. Writing celebrations are extended as students receive responses to their writing via comments, as well as when we share reflections and joys of the daily writing life.

Don't make blogging more complicated than it needs to be. Determine the purpose of your blog. Is it only to share learning from writing workshop, or do you want to share other parts of the school day too? Also, decide on a regular posting schedule. Like most things, the success of your blog lies in a regular commitment. When can people expect to see updates? For example, you may decide to blog every Monday, Wednesday, and Friday. Or perhaps you'll update every Thursday. The important thing is that updates should happen at least once a week at a predictable time. Readers of your classroom blog will be more likely to make a habit of checking in to see what's new if they know you'll be making updates regularly.

Twitter

When we began using Twitter in classrooms, little did we know how much we would emphasize grammar. In fact, because of Twitter, we taught more conventions than ever before. Are you thinking *Really? Teaching more grammar with 140 characters in a forum where Standard English is often abandoned?* Yes, more grammar than before.

Although Standard English is often sidestepped, the reason is the parameters of Twitter. Twitter is a form of microblogging; you must post your message using no more than 140 characters, including spaces between words. When we use Twitter in the classroom, we type the message conventionally first. If the message is more than 140 characters, we discuss how to make it shorter. Often we change the sentence structure to say the same thing, but in a more concise way. Sometimes we remove instances of *and* and use commas or ampersands instead. And from time to time we change a *you* to *u* or a *too* to *2*.

These deviations from Standard English are used as a last resort and with the understanding that it is to save characters to make the tweet possible.

At the end of writing workshop, we often share our learning with our Tweeps. For example, we might want to tweet this:

> Today we learned authors use the five senses (ex. touch, taste, sight, smell, and hearing) in their illustrations and words to make their stories come alive for the audience.

This tweet is 174 characters—way too many for Twitter. So we begin shrinking it by first considering a way to be more concise. We might change it to this:

> Authors use five senses (touch, taste, sight, smell, hearing) in illustrations and words to make their stories come alive for the audience.

Now the tweet is 139 characters. It is almost exactly at the character limit; however, if any one wanted to retweet our message, he or she would be over the limit. So we need to cut it down a little more. Next we check for more places we can cut as well as places to use commas or ampersands.

> Authors use five senses (touch, taste, sight, smell, hearing) in illustrations & words to make their stories come alive.

Now we are at 119 characters. Before hitting send, we will reread it one more time!

It is important to reread tweets before they become public. This provides another opportunity to remind students that when you put something on the Internet, anyone can see it and it is a reflection of you.

When we decide what to tweet, we have many conversations about what kinds of "unsaid" messages our tweets might send. Will people think we are complaining? Will they know we are joking, or will our message sound rude?

During the share session in writing workshop, we often tweet meaningful responses students receive about their writing, reflections students have shared, or the highlights of our successes. (See examples in Figure 3.3.) Quickly and easily we extend the writing celebrations happening daily to an online community.

I learned readers love to know the inside story so I added thought bubbles.

My writing group thought my new ending was funny.

When I didn't know what to write, I looked through my writer's notebook for ideas.

Figure 3.3 Our tweets might sound like these.

During formal writing celebrations, we often tweet favorite lines from students' writing projects or favorite responses students receive. We celebrate both the process of being writers and the products. Often when student writing is shared via a blog post, we tweet a link to the blog post in order to share with even more people. (A note about online privacy: Our blog and Twitter accounts are as private as possible. Twitter followers must be approved by us, and all comments on the blog are moderated before being approved for posting. Anyone can view our blog, but only approved friends can comment. Only classrooms, authors, parents, and former students are permitted to follow us on Twitter.)

Facebook

The purpose of social networks is communication. If we want effective communication with families, then we need to reach them in the spaces they already inhabit. Many adults are consistent Facebook users, so it makes sense to create a classroom Facebook page. This allows us to meet parents on their turf, making it easier for them to be involved with our classrooms.

Writing celebrations can be extended to Facebook when we post photos and status updates that share responses, reflections, and rejoicing during the celebration. On Facebook, we can also share links to blog posts that highlight writing celebrations.

Skype (or Google Hangout)

Skype provides an opportunity to talk face-to-face with people in other places. We can Skype with classrooms in our own school district, or in another state, or on another continent. It is essential to plan ahead and determine a time and topic for the Skype conversation. Through Twitter, Christi connected with a classroom in Ireland. They arranged to have a transatlantic writing celebration. Each classroom posted their writing on their blogs. Then they offered responses through comments. They shared reflections via Twitter. Finally, each classroom put together a box of candy to send across the globe. The rejoicing portion of the celebration took place as they taste-tested candy from the other country. Everything was organized, planned, and implemented through social networks. Ultimately, they Skyped with one another, finally getting to "meet" face-to-face.

Many authors offer free Skype visits with classrooms. Check out the list of authors offering Skype visits online at Skype an Author Network (http://skypeanauthor.wikifoundry.com/). By organizing a Skype visit with an author who is a writing mentor, the energy for writing is increased. Skype extends writing celebrations and gives students experiences that would be impossible without this social media.

Google Hangout is an alternative to Skype. It is easy to use and allows you to "meet" with more than one person at a time. As long as you have a Google account, you have access to Google Hangouts.

YouTube

YouTube offers a place to share videos. You can upload videos of your own and then share with others the links to the videos on

YouTube. This makes it possible to extend writing celebrations to families who are unable to attend a school-day celebration. It also allows other classrooms from around the globe to celebrate virtually alongside you.

YouTube is also an excellent resource for finding short videos about authors' processes. Using the search box on the site you can type in an author's name and have interviews, process videos, and book trailers at your fingertips.

Pinterest

Pinterest is a resource that can help teachers connect to others and find even more ways to extend writing celebrations. Pinterest is a place to collect images. People tag images with keywords to make them manageable. You can find many ideas for ways to respond, reflect, and rejoice with student writers. As with other social networks, you are able to follow other users on Pinterest. Look for teachers to follow and begin building a network of reliable resources.

Envisioning Your Online Space

There are many ways to celebrate writers in your classroom, but shrinking the world for them via your classroom's own online space is a powerful way to help them celebrate. Going global can fuel writers in new and important ways. If you choose to create an online space for writers, it's critical to keep a focused picture in your mind of what kind of space you want it to be and how you want your students to use it.

Begin by visiting the networking sites outlined in Figure 3.2. Notice the people or classrooms you enjoy visiting and want to visit again. What is appealing to you about their sites or accounts? Why do you like to visit them? I appreciate visiting people who are positive, genuine, and generous. I like getting new ideas, and I enjoy feeling grateful to be an educator after I visit someone's online space. What do you want others to say about you and your class after they visit you online? Let this vision inspire your posts and the things you decide to share, lifting celebrations to a new level that is unattainable without technology. Figure 3.4 can help you begin to envision your online space.

> - How will this space help my students grow and celebrate their writing lives?
> - How can I organize this space so it is student centered?
> - How often do I want to maintain the space?
> - How will I direct students and parents to useful information on the web for writers?
> - How will the online space reflect what I value in my students?

Figure 3.4 When creating an online space through which your writers can celebrate, consider the questions listed here.

Your responses to these questions will help you decide where to establish a presence in an online community. Go ahead and join a community. As you become steeped in the community, it will become more obvious how to use the network as a place to celebrate the writers in your classroom.

It Takes Time

In order to participate in an online community for writing celebrations, we must have tenacity. Many online spaces only reach their potential once you are connected to a network of other teachers, classrooms, writers, and experts. As with face-to-face networks, it takes time to build relationships online. Relationships are built when others realize you are responsible and active in the online community.

Remember, you don't have to do it all in one year. There are some options which can be a single event. A Skype visit could be done once a school year, for example. Take a look at the possibilities for an online space and choose one to establish in your classroom.

As your class participates in this forum, look for opportunities to connect worldwide and to teach the digital natives in your classroom ways to use social networks in effective and responsible ways. Figure 3.5 lists some suggestions to help you keep your participation in online communities productive and valuable for you and your students.

- These sites are not places to vent about students, nor are they a place for students to complain.
- Continually ask yourself: "How is this helping my students learn?"
- Connect with as many people as you can, as safely as you can. Keep yourself aware of everything that's happening with all of your online interactions. Look for opportunities to talk with students about Internet safety.

Figure 3.5 A Few Things to Keep in Mind

Hesitations

Communication with parents about our classroom use of digital tools is critical. It is our responsibility to communicate not only the kinds of digital tools we are using in the classroom but also the purpose of each. Consider using Figure 3.2 as a way to describe the reasons you are using specific tools in your classroom. You can use a table or a letter to communicate with parents.

As we enter into online spaces, it is important to teach Internet safety. Tweens and teens are prime targets for online predators. By beginning conversations in the early grades and continuing these conversations throughout elementary school, we can help students be proactive in protecting themselves. When we use digital tools alongside students, we also invite parents into the conversation. This helps raise awareness in homes and gives families the opportunity to continue conversations with their children.

An initial conversation with families about the level of online sharing they are willing to allow for their child is necessary. Figure 3.6 shows a sample letter to families describing the different online spaces. Check the Internet use policies specific to your school and be diligent in following them for the safety of your students.

Social media is not a media. The key is to listen, engage, and build relationships.

—*David Alston*

Dear Families and Friends of Room _____,

It is likely that when our children grow up they will be part of an online community, so it is important they learn how to be *kind and responsible contributors* in online spaces. Our classroom is one place for students to learn how to interact with others online.

We will be active in a number of online communities. It is my hope that you will join us in some of these spaces. Below you will find our online stomping grounds, how to follow us, and the purposes of the spaces.

Rest assured, I have checked the Internet Privacy form you completed during school registration and will respect your wishes for the online use of your child's picture, name, and work. If at any time you change your mind regarding your decision, please let me know.

If you have any questions, please don't hesitate to ask.

Hoping to see you online,

Teacher Name

Online Space	How to Follow Us	Our Purpose
Twitter @username	You can see our tweets by accessing our timeline. You can follow and respond to our tweets by creating your own Twitter account.	We will tweet our learning, updates on classroom happenings, and things we are curious about. We will also connect to other classrooms, authors, and organizations.
Blog Blog Address	Go to our blog by entering the address in your web browser. The most recent post will be at the top.	We will share scans of our writing, classroom photos, and the weekly newsletter.
Facebook Page Name	Like our Facebook page in order to see updates.	The main purpose of our Facebook page is communication with families. We will share links to blog posts, reminders, and classroom information. This information is also available via the paper copy of the class newsletter.

Figure 3.6 This sample letter to families outlines how to find the class in different online spaces as well as the purpose behind each online space.

By establishing social networking sites as learning environments, doors open for our students. We also believe in offering an invitation to families to join us in online networks. When families begin following you on your blog, Facebook, and Twitter, they will offer encouragement to the class. At the same time they will receive the added benefit of having an insider's perspective on the learning happening in the classroom. As parents see the value in using social networks, they are able to scaffold and support their children as they grow and become contributing members in a variety of online spaces.

The best way to teach students how to use their online voices responsibly is to begin engaging in the global society alongside our students. As we do this, more doors open for ways to extend writing celebrations, and our students' voices are heard in powerful ways.

CHAPTER 4

FORMAL CELEBRATIONS

When someone says something nice about my book it makes me feel good. It makes me want to keep on making my books better.

—Wesley Hays, age 8

Celebrating the process is essential to every writer's life. It fuels us and keeps us going on the tough days. We realize what works best for us and what can be changed to make our process more effective. We learn things about ourselves as writers, and, more important, we come to understandings about ourselves as humans.

Of course, the writing process leads to a product. As writers we make *something,* and this something ought to be shared. Expanding writing celebrations may mean stretching ourselves to relish in the accomplishment of creating a final product. From time to time, we host formal writing celebrations. These are genuine celebrations, encompassing response, reflection, and rejoicing. Preparing writing to go public is part of the writing process and something students ought to experience. Formal writing celebrations are another building block in celebrating students' writing lives.

I was working in Deborah Nelson's kindergarten classroom with a focus on telling stories across pages, and students were creating books. The teaching points were bubbling up organically out of what students were doing as writers. During several mini-lessons the students were the teachers. We learned about making our illustrations show how a character was feeling on the inside with posture, facial expressions, and color. We learned about revising, and we learned about adding sentences to help tell the story. Students were content and happy writers. But Deborah and I felt like their best was missing. They were doing well. They were trying. But it seemed a little lackluster.

The unit was coming to an end, so we began planning for an end-of-unit celebration. Since we were celebrating the process throughout the unit, we decided to focus the celebration on their favorite books. We asked them which story, of all the stories they'd written, they would like to share with others.

"What do you mean share with others?" one student asked.

"We're going to invite some guests and then share our books with them. We want to share our favorite work with them so they can see how much we know as writers." There was a buzz in the meeting area as the excitement settled in. "So how will we know a book is done?" I asked. "How can we tell it is our best work?"

We began a chart (Figure 4.1) and over the next several days used the chart to ensure the books students chose for the celebration were complete and ready. In the writing center, Deborah set up a celebration box where students placed their books when they were ready for the celebration. She added a laminated class list to the front of the box, and students and checked off their names using a dry-erase marker when their books were in the box. This system allowed us to know at a glance who was still preparing for the celebration. With each book added to the box, their excitement continued to rise.

More important, the quality of work rose. Deborah and I paged through the books in the celebration box and gushed over the meaningful work. This was what we were expecting. It made my heart patter a little faster, because I could see tracks of learning and I knew their books were their best work. It made me realize that if we only celebrate process, we miss out on a prime opportunity to lift the quality of writing. We miss out on seeing what our students are capable of doing as writers.

Formal celebrations provide an opportunity for us to share our very best work with an audience. Audience matters—both the community of writers within our classroom walls and the audience beyond the classroom. When preparing for a formal celebration, in addition

Figure 4.1 This anchor chart helps younger students clarify whether their work is ready for a formal celebration.

to considering response, reflection, and rejoicing, we also need to consider audience. Who is going to celebrate alongside the writers in our classrooms and encourage them to sustain their writing lives?

Realizing this was a crucial shift in my thinking. We could celebrate our lives as writers and the products we created. At the beginning of my understanding of writing workshop, I viewed formal writing celebrations as a way to "show off" the students' work. I wanted to awe the audience and make people think I was a miracle worker. I dreamed of parents, administrators, and colleagues saying, "Look what students can do after they are in writing workshop with Mrs. Ayres. Their writing is amazing." (You must know, I'm ducking my head with embarrassment as I share this with you.)

But it wasn't all about me. I wanted students to feel a sense of accomplishment and pride in their work. I wanted them to gain confidence as writers and to believe they could accomplish great tasks. I was mistaken in believing that creating a perfect product would accomplish these goals.

I've learned, however, that accomplishing the goals of building confidence and nudging growth requires us to stay focused on the writer. We need to angle the audience's attention toward the intentional work writers are doing—or almost doing, or attempting to do. For our celebration in Deborah's room, a handful of guests joined us. Before students shared their books, we said to the audience, "Check out the characters in the stories and see if you can figure out what they are feeling on the inside. Ask the writers what they did *purposefully* to make the emotions obvious to the reader." We also said, "We've been learning that writers revise. You might want to find out what the writers in your group did to revise their books and why they made those choices."

The focus remains on the writer, and the celebration is genuine. It is not orchestrated to show off work, but to continue the journey as writers. Planning a formal celebration often begins with determining the audience and then considering how response, reflection, and rejoicing will stream out from there. There are three ways to share the joy of writing with others.

1. We can celebrate with our writing community and invite guests to join us in our classroom.
2. We can put our writing into the community in the form of a local celebration outside of the school building.
3. We can go global and share our writing digitally with others around the world.

You don't have to do all three right now, but do consider expanding the writing celebrations with your students to include a larger audience.

Celebrating as a Community

The strength of learning to write in writing workshop is the community of writers that support one another. No longer is writing about the teacher telling students how to do it; it is about everyone living writing lives. It is impossible to work shoulder to shoulder with other writers and not develop a community. It is an organic process and happens naturally when writers are together. Celebration happens mostly within this community as we put stories and opinions and information on the page day in and day out. From time to time, it is important to step away from the daily grind and celebrate the writing we create. Even though we are sharing our best work in formal celebrations, we are still taking care to create genuine celebrations through response, reflection, and rejoicing as a community of writers.

Response

The responses in formal writing community celebrations will come primarily from classmates. However, it is also appropriate to invite other guests. Consider teachers (who may be on prep during your celebration time), other classes, administrators, and support staff. You may ask the superintendent, curriculum director, custodian, cook, nurse, or secretary. Who do your students interact with during the school day? These are the perfect people to invite to a celebration. One of my favorite guests is Matt Pulley, a music teacher, because he is a writer. He responds as a writer, and kids are always encouraged. They are able to see what it looks like to be a lifelong writer. Mr. Pulley doesn't publish books, but he is a writer. This is the kind of writer our students will most likely grow up to be. I'm sure you can find this kind of gem in your school too. You'll never know unless you open your formal celebrations to guests.

Reflection

For formal celebrations, reflection may occur before, during, or after the celebration. When reflection happens before the celebration, students are able to consider how their writing process influenced the final product. They can think ahead and then plan to share an understanding about their writing process during the celebration.

One way to encourage reflection during the celebration is with a list of questions to spur discussion about each person's writing process. You'll find several question lists throughout this book.

Another possibility is to reflect after the writing celebration. When reflection is saved until this point, students are able to consider how formal celebration influences their writing lives.

There are advantages to each of the timing options. We can be intentional about timing reflections at different points in formal celebrations throughout the course of the school year. This way we can tap the advantages of each.

Rejoicing

We've pushed ourselves to consider ways to rejoice in formal celebrations beyond the traditional inclusion of food. At the beginning of the year, it's a good idea to have an author photo shoot. We sometimes gather "writerly" attire by collecting hats, ties, and scarves, and then we have students select their props and pose for an author photo. Students are able to plan ahead and dress for their author photo because we talk about the photo shoot ahead of time. By posting the photos with students' first reflections, you have the makings of an instant bulletin board. You can update this board throughout the year by posting current writing projects or updated reflections. Just like online spaces for celebration, this bulletin board becomes a space within your classroom (or school) for celebrating writers.

Students also enjoy writer goodie bags as part of a formal celebration. Some of our favorite goodies include small candies or mints as well as pencils, gel pens, stickers, and miniature notebooks. Disposable cameras make it easy for students to document bits of their lives for their notebooks. For our youngest writers, we've included blank books and colored pencils. We think goodie bags are perfect for a celebration prior to a school break. Students return after time away and share the ways they used their goodie bag contents to continue to live as writers even though they weren't in school. They can't wait to share the way they filled new notebooks, added photos to their writer's notebooks, or wrote a new book. This is the power of a celebration to inspire students to become lifelong writers.

Another way we've rejoiced is through costume. During our nonfiction writing celebration, students share information about their topic orally. We explain to students that when we present information to others, we dress professionally. We ask students to consider how an expert of their topic would dress. Students then dress up as experts from their fields. Dirt bike riders (with suits and helmets), gymnasts, and animal researchers have all joined us for a formal celebration (Figure 4.2). Other students have dressed professionally by wearing dresses or button-down shirts with ties. Their costumes show a deeper understanding of the way experts share information about a topic as well as adding another dimension to rejoicing during the celebration.

Figure 4.2 Christi's second-grade students dressed up for the formal nonfiction writing celebration.

Putting Writing into the Local Community

It is one thing to invite people into the school, but there are many community members who are interested in the work students are doing but don't have the opportunity to come to the school. Many parents work during the school day, and many people who don't have students still care about the youngest members of the local community. Still others had a negative school experience and are uncomfortable entering school buildings. It is important to expand writing celebrations to include the local community.

By framing student work and displaying it in community businesses, we infiltrate the community with our writing. We put together class anthologies and students give them to local doctor's offices when they go to appointments. Students write letters to the editor of the local paper. We encourage students to enter writing contests. As we put writing into the community, it's with the intent of celebrating by going public. Therefore, we still question, How can we broaden genuine celebration of writers outside of the walls of our classrooms?

Response

As we send writing out into the world, it is difficult to predict the responses it will receive. Most likely, responses will happen informally as our students cross paths with people who have read their writing. By developing a system for students to share these responses, we are able to capture it and share it. A bulletin board titled "What They're Saying About Us as Writers" creates a space to document responses from the nonschool community. Students can post notes about the responses they've received to their writing. Often the local newspaper features a writing celebration, or someone posts a letter to the editor about our writing work. When this happens, we clip these articles and add them to the bulletin board. Other times a family member or guest from a writing celebration will send a note, and we post these too. We are intentional about creating a space to capture community responses, making students more attuned to it when they do receive a response.

Reflection

It's important to provide students with an opportunity to consider how making their work public influences them as writers. How were they motivated as writers? Did their writing process change as they considered putting their work into the community? We have the opportunity to tap into considerations when reflecting on sharing our work with the local community. It is important to provide time for this reflection.

Rejoicing

The act of taking an anthology to a doctor's office is joyful. When we donate a framed piece of writing to a local business we rejoice. (And we rejoice again and again when we go into businesses and see our writing or classmates' writing on display.) When we shake open the newspaper and face student writing, we rejoice. It is these simple acts of joy that fuel our writers.

Formal Writing Celebrations Go Global

Once you've established online spaces for celebrating the daily grind of the writers in your classroom, you can use this same space for formal celebrations. We've expanded our thinking about formal celebrations by capturing images, voice recordings, and videos to share with the global community. Sharing in a more formal way via the online space you've established gives students an even greater audience.

Response

Most often the responses to our global celebrations come as comments to blog posts or responses to tweets. Students are fueled to continue writing when they receive these responses. You may consider creating a bulletin board titled "Our Global Community" and posting two maps, one of the United States and another of the world. You will probably have many responses from across the United States, so it is nice to be able to identify the states. Then, by printing the comments, you can attach them to the maps, identifying the location of the members of your global community. This space for responses helps students gain a sense of geography while at the same time realizing that their voices can influence others.

Reflection

Helping students to consider how their voices are influencing people across the globe is an important component for global celebrations. Students can forget that their words impact others when they're sitting behind a computer screen. Online bullying is rampant for this reason. Often students become bold and lash out at others because they feel they have the protection of the elusive cyberspace. Global celebrations help dispel this myth. Global celebrations help students realize the personal nature of social networking, and they experience the way their words influence others and how the responses of others impact them.

Rejoicing

More and more I've been turning to Pinterest to expand the rejoicing during celebrations. My daughter asked to bring cookies to her writing celebration, so I found inspiration for pencil sugar cookies online. I pinned the image and shared it via Pinterest. Soon the community of teachers who follow me on Pinterest were repinning the image and envisioning using this idea to rejoice in their classrooms. I find ideas not only for treats and drinks but also for goodie bags, writer gifts, and bulletin boards. I'm always impressed by how the more I give to an online community, the more I get. I try to *outgive* the community, but it is proving impossible.

No matter the audience for the celebration, make a plan for how to respond, reflect, and rejoice as writers. Consider using the planning guide in Figure 4.3 as well as the ideas in Chapter 5 to think through an upcoming formal celebration.

Formal Celebration Planning Guide

What have students been working on as writers?

Determine the audience for the celebration.

- Classroom
- Local
- Global

Determine the focus of the celebration.

- Process
- Product

Make a plan for **genuine** celebration!

We will receive responses by . . .	We will reflect as writers by . . .	We will rejoice by . . .

TO-DO List

- Celebration Date _____
-
-
-
-

Figure 4.3 Formal Celebration Planning Guide

CHAPTER 5

FORTY FORMAL
CELEBRATION IDEAS

I like it when we celebrate big.
—Allie Haberman, age 8

Here are forty formal writing celebrations, organized according to how much time you have to prepare. By stretching your creative muscles, you can imagine how to incorporate response, reflection, and rejoicing within each celebration idea.

I Need a Formal Celebration Idea for Tomorrow

1. **Silent Celebration:** Each student displays their writing and a response sheet (Figure 5.1). Students move from space to space, reading and responding in silence. At the end, students rejoice by reading their comments and then sharing one or two of their favorite responses with the whole class.

2. **Small-Group Celebration:** Students share their writing and offer responses and reflections in a small group of three to five writers.

_____

Please leave an encouraging comment.

Figure 5.1 Response Sheet

3. **Toast:** In *Independent Writing*, Colleen Cruz (2003) suggests that writers gather with small glasses of juice and that the teacher offer a toast to the writers. You can toast to their learning, to their success in completing their writing projects, and to the community of writers. "Here! Here!" the writers say, and then the floor is open to anyone who wants to share about the impact of writing workshop.

4. **In-Progress Celebration:** Students bring their writer's notebooks and draft folders and share their in-progress work during a celebration.

5. **Notebook Celebrations:** In this celebration, the focus is on writer's notebooks and the way they influence our writing lives. Prior to the celebration, students reflect on their notebook entries and select two to four notebook pages they would like to share with others. At the end of the celebration, students rejoice by tapping into the inspiration they found during the celebration and create new notebook entries.

6. **Classroom Library Celebrations:** Make a basket for student books in the classroom library. It is powerful when students see their books alongside published authors. Plus, students enjoy reading their own books as well as their classmates' books. Figures 5.2 and 5.3 share two possible choices for a label to add to a basket in your classroom library.

7. **Lunch Table Writing:** Students scatter their writing on lunch tables, along with a response sheet like the one in Figure 5.1, so other students can offer feedback. Plastic sheet protectors or laminating will help protect the work from sloppy eaters!

Figures 5.2 & 5.3 Possible book bin labels for the classroom library

8. **Alfresco Celebration:** Take the celebration outside and offer opening remarks referring to "the fresh air and fresh writing we are sharing today." Students proceed to share their writing with small groups.

9. **Author's Chair:** If you make a special chair for writers, you can use it if you are crunched for time to plan a celebration. Students take turns sitting in the Author's Chair and read aloud a portion of their writing, and then others offer oral or written responses. For the chair itself you can paint a flea-market find or be creative: milk jugs, paint buckets, and old rocking chairs all hold writers up in celebration. Check out Figure 5.4 for a collection of Author's Chairs.

Figure 5.4 Classroom Author's Chairs

10. **Writing Process Celebration:** Students share the way *they* use the writing process. Often a list of questions, like the one in Figure 5.5, is helpful to guide the discussion of in-progress work.

Writing Process Questions: Intermediate Grades

- How does your writer's notebook help you plan your writing?

- What makes drafting go well for you?

- What is the easiest part of the writing process for you?

- How did you revise?

- What tools did you use to edit your writing for conventions?

- How did other writers help you with your project?

- Who are you excited to share your writing with?

Figure 5.5 Writing Process Questions

11. **Across-Grade-Level Celebration:** Students share their writer's notebooks, draft folders, or final products with students from another grade level. They often enjoy sharing in small groups.

12. **Goodie Bag Celebration:** Writers love writing supplies! Gather a few special writing tools, small notebooks, and stickers in brown lunch sacks. For primary writers, include a few unlined blank books. Prior to a break is a great time for this celebration, because you will send your students home with excitement and tools to write.

13. **Poetry Jam:** Each student brings a poem to the celebration. Sit in a circle and have one person begin by reading his or her poem. The next person to read is determined by linking his or her poem to the previous poem. For example, if the first reader shares a poem about playing ball with her dog, then the next reader might also have a dog poem. Or perhaps the next reader makes a connection by saying, "Your dog likes to play with a ball and my poem is about baseball." The object is to connect each poem to the previous

one in some way. Be creative and remember that poets often snap rather than clap to show their appreciation for a poem.

14. **Writers Helping Writers:** In this celebration, students determine something they would like to have feedback about in regard to their current writing project. For example, a student may bring two different leads to the celebration in order to figure out which one is most effective. Perhaps a student is concerned about whether there are enough facts in the informative article he or she is writing. A student may be wondering whether his or her opinions are clear in a persuasive letter. For the celebration, students bring their issues and gather feedback from other writers. Figure 5.6 shows a Writers Helping Writers form to help students organize their thoughts and gather feedback.

Writers Helping Writers

Name: _____   Date:_____

Current Writing Project _____

- -

The new thing I'm learning about myself as a writer is _____

_____

In this project something I'm trying as a writer is _____

_____

Read your draft and consider a section or issue you would like feedback on.

I'd like to know _____

_____

What others are saying…

Figure 5.6 Writers Helping Writers Form

15. **Traveling Notebook:** This is a writer's notebook designed to travel from home to home. It is a great way for students to get to know one another as well as for family members to experience collecting ideas as writers. When the notebook returns to the classroom, writers share the pages they added at home. Then the notebook goes home with another student. In Figure 5.7 you will find a note and list to tape into the front of the notebook to help families understand what to collect in the notebook. You may also want to consider decorating the notebook cover as a class.

Traveling Writer's Notebook

Hello,

You and your family are invited to add to our class notebook. A writer's notebook is a place to collect the "stuff" of life. It is a lifeline for a writer. Students keep their own notebooks, but we also thought it would be useful to have a notebook created by our community. The purpose is to create a resource we can use to jump-start our creativity and help us find ideas for writing projects. Feel free to create a page (or more) together as a family.

Things to CATCH in Our Writer's Notebook

Memories	Questions	Current Events
Maps	Dreams	Artifacts
Words	Funny Things	Photographs
Lists	Collections	Magazine Clippings
Feelings	Cards	Comics
Drawings	Quotes	Newspaper Clippings

If your family is anything like most families, you probably don't have time to add one more thing to do. Please keep this simple. Leave the notebook out where your family will see it. The kitchen counter, the coffee table, or even the car are all possibilities. Set out a few writing utensils and a roll of tape. Then let the magic happen. Tape in the ticket stubs from the high school game. Add a wrapper from your favorite candy and write why it makes your mouth happy. Jot a list of common phrases people say in your house. Make a page that captures the sounds in your kitchen. Feel free to add as few or as many pages as you want. We're just happy to have a bit of your life as inspiration for us as writers.

Figure 5.7 Traveling Writer's Notebook Letter to Families

16. **Bulletin Board:** Students complete a reflection like the one in Figure 5.8 for a bulletin board and then display their writing next to it. By using page protectors or plastic frames, students are easily able to change the writing they display throughout the year. Also consider including a letter from you, the teacher, to the viewer of the bulletin board directing attention to the learning writers are experiencing. This will help keep the focus off of conventional errors. For sample letters, check out Figures 5.9 and 5.10.

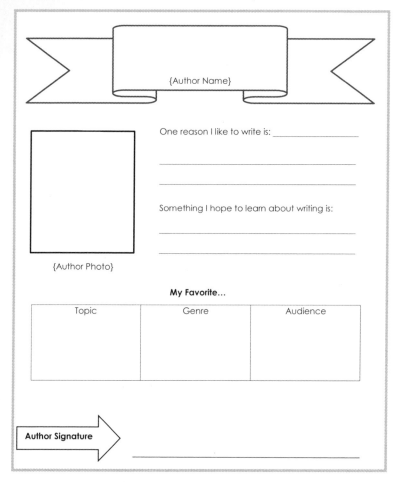

Figure 5.8 Student Reflection for Bulletin Board Display

Can You Spot Our Learning?

Thanks for taking the time to read our stories!
We've been practicing lots of things as writers.
See if you can spot what we've been learning to do as writers.

Our illustrations . . .

Fill the page

Show setting

Include characters

Show action

Our words . . .

Label important parts in the illustration

Use letters to make sounds

Include the first and last sound

Figure 5.9 Letter to Viewers of Primary-Grade Writing Celebration Bulletin Boards

17. **Author Interviews:** Students plan to interview their writing partners for the celebration. The writing process question list in Figure 5.5 and the interview question list in Figure 2.12 are good places for students to begin planning their interviews. This celebration allows students to understand the writing process in a more personal way. Plan to share a few interviews each day across a week or two. To go all out, stage a "talk show" atmosphere with unique chairs and microphones. Another option is to video record the interviews and share them via YouTube.

18. **Placemats:** Students turn their favorite family stories into placemats by taking an oversized sheet of construction paper, adding their stories and illustrations, and then laminating them. This unique publishing opportunity allows students the opportunity to share writing with their families. It is also a great springboard

Can You Spot Our Learning?

Thanks for taking the time to read our feature articles! We've been learning how to write informative text by using research and craft strategies. See if you can spot what we've been learning to do as writers.

Research . . .

Use credible sources

Share important facts

Teach using a variety of facts, such as descriptions, statistics, and anecdotes

Craft . . .

Hook the reader's curiosity in the beginning

Use subtopics to organize information

Weave facts into own words

Conventions . . .

Organize ideas with paragraphs

Capitalize proper nouns

Quote a source using quotation marks

Figure 5.10 Letter to Viewers of Upper-Grade Writing Celebration Bulletin Boards

for families to share other memories. Consider giving students time at school to share their families' reactions.

19. **Framing Writing for Local Businesses:** Young writers' stories are often exquisite when displayed in a frame. The whimsy of the illustration and words is perfect for local businesses. Consider using several frames to share each page of a book or to share several students' projects.

20. **Classroom Anthologies in Doctor's Offices:** Older students can compile anthologies of their stories, articles, letters, or

poems. Students can determine themes for the anthologies and then submit writing for the compilation, or you can compile an anthology at the end of a unit of study. We always had one or two anthologies waiting for students to take with them when they left for a doctor's appointment. Consider writing a letter to the reader and attaching it to the anthology, similar to the bulletin board letter in Figure 5.10, to highlight the writing moves students have made. Nudged this way, anthology readers will be less likely to focus on the errors.

I Have Plenty of Time to Plan a Formal Celebration

21. **Joint Writing Workshop:** Plan to celebrate with another classroom. It is best to consider how you will group students before the day of the celebration. With a little planning, you could consider a rotation for the celebration. At the beginning of one school year, two second-grade classrooms and two third-grade classrooms joined together for a celebration. Students rotated through the four classrooms. In one classroom, they *responded* by reading and jotting a note on a comment form in a silent celebration. In another classroom they *rejoiced* by getting their author photo taken for the bulletin board. We gathered many props, such as hats, scarves, and ties, for them to use in their photos. A third classroom in the rotation was for *reflection*. Here, a teacher offered a toast, and students shared their learning as writers. The fourth classroom held a second *reflection* experience, where students completed reflection sheets as shown in Figure 5.8.

22. **Mentor Author Celebration:** Consider sharing the inspiration of a mentor author in conjunction with student work. In her kindergarten classroom, Tonya Haywood displays a page from a book by Eric Carle alongside her students' books. She also displays a written explanation about how the students write like Eric Carle. Tonya creates a PowerPoint presentation by scanning student

work to share on the big screen with parents and students. You can join Deborah Nelson's kindergarten students in a Mentor Author Celebration by viewing their YouTube video showing how Mo Willems inspired them. (See Figure 3.1 on page 39.)

23. **Expert Writing Celebration:** After an informational writing project, students dress up as experts in their fields and deliver oral presentations. In one second-grade class, students wrote "all-about" books on topics of their choice. We scanned their covers and then offered them note cards like the one in Figure 5.11 to support their presentations. They completed their cards and then delivered their short presentations from a microphone in the school's theater, with the cover of their book displayed behind them. At the end of the presentations, guests were invited back to the classroom to read the books. Guests offered oral responses and rejoiced over cookies and punch. Figure 5.12 shows Allie and me dressed as writers for the Expert Writing Celebration. Allie wrote a book titled *Everything You Need to Know to Be a Writer.*

24. **Campfire Celebration:** Stories love to dance around a campfire. Either real or pretend, set up a campfire and give students a

My name is _____. I studied _____.

One cool fact about my topic is: _____

_____.

An important fact about my topic is: _____

_____.

Thank you.

(smile)

Figure 5.11 Students can fill out note cards like this to support their oral presentations.

Figure 5.12 Ruth and Allie dressed as writers for the Expert Writing Celebration

chance to share their stories. Of course, s'mores are a perfect way to rejoice during this kind of celebration. Students may share—or complete—reflections in addition to sharing their stories. For a list of reflection questions about narrative writing, see Figure 5.13.

Thinking about our writing lives . . .

1. What is your favorite part of your narrative?

2. What did you do well as a storyteller?

3. What do you know about yourself as a writer that you didn't know before?

4. What's the next narrative you want to write?

5. What do you still want to learn about writing stories?

Figure 5.13 Reflection Questions for Narrative Writing

25. **Poetry Café:** In beatnik style, plan a poetry café. Students will need some time to prepare to recite their poems aloud. If possible, set up a mic and invite students to dress in beatnik attire (black turtlenecks, berets). Celebrate the beatnik time period. Smoothies are a kid-friendly alternative to coffee.

26. **Family Writing Workshop:** Invite families to attend an after-school writing workshop. Plan a mini-lesson. (See one of my favorite mini-lesson ideas in Figure 5.14; more are available on this book's accompanying website, www.stenhouse.com/celebratingwriters.) Then give families a chance to write together —feel free to confer and talk with families as they write. End the workshop with a share session, first giving families a chance to share together and then inviting writers to share with the whole group. When scheduled near the beginning of the year, this celebration provides an opportunity to help parents understand and experience writing workshop.

27. **Take-Home Celebration:** Set up celebration folders in which students can take home their writing. Create a letter like the one in Figure 5.15 to help students reflect as writers and to help parents rejoice in the learning. Sometimes, if the genre is short—for example, reviews or poetry—you may consider having students select more than one to share with their families. Use the completed notes and the favorite reviews to create a bulletin board.

28. **Writing as Gifts:** Students consider the way they can give their writing as a gift. Writing can be rolled and tied with a ribbon, placed in a thick envelope, or framed before wrapping. During the celebration, students *reflect* on the way audience has impacted their writing. They *rejoice* by wrapping the gift of writing and later share the response they were given about their gift.

29. **Performances:** Mitch Willaman invites his fifth-grade students to research a person of interest and then prepare to share their learning in a Wax Museum. Keith Bollman, another fifth-grade teacher, empowers his students to share their learning about the solar system by creating an interactive tour for classrooms and the community. Performances and exhibits provide opportunities to connect writing workshop to other content areas.

Make a Storyboard

Stories are a collection of scenes. Families can plan the scenes of their story by sketching or jotting on a storyboard. This makes it possible for them to each write a different scene of the story, and then put it together as a whole. For a fun twist to the evening, ask families to consider different orders to their scenes, giving them a chance to get creative with the structure, moving beyond chronological.

Figure 5.14 Possible Mini-Lesson for Family Writing Night

30. **Writing and Dessert Night:** This makes a wonderful schoolwide celebration. Classrooms share their writing either through bulletin boards or by displaying writing projects on students' desks.

Review Writing Celebration

We've been working on writing reviews. Here are two of my favorites. Two things I've learned about sharing my opinion in a review are:

1. _____

2. _____

One thing I'm proud of about writing reviews is:

1. _____

We've been learning that reviews **influence** people. Please write a response below so I know how my writing impacts you.

Figure 5.15 Sample note to include in a take-home celebration folder

Comment sheets invite a response from families and friends. Work with parent-teacher organizations or local businesses to provide a dessert bar so families can rejoice with writers.

31. **Fancy Publishing:** Katie Wood Ray and Lisa Cleveland discuss fancy publishing in their book *About the Authors* (2003). They suggest arranging for parent volunteers to help primary students type their books. You can then print the pages, giving space for illustrations. This is something extra special that might happen

once a year. Perhaps consider offering fancy publishing as an option for a handful of students each unit.

32. Growth Celebration: In this celebration, students bring two writing projects with the intention of showing their growth. They share a reflection about how they have grown as a writer, using the differences between the earlier and later pieces of writing as evidence. This reflection can be oral, or you can use the Growth Reflection Sheet in Figure 5.16.

Name   Date

About Writing

I used to think writing was . . .

Now I think writing is . . .

About Conventions

One new thing I've learned about conventions is . . .

About Craft

My favorite way to work the words is . . .

About Process

I'm effective as a writer when I . . .

About Change

The biggest difference between the way I used to write and the way I write now is . . .

Figure 5.16 Growth Reflection Sheet

33. Best Book Ever Celebration: Primary students consider all of the books they've written during the school year and select one to revise, molding it into their best book ever. Older students could have a version of this celebration by selecting their favorite writing project and revising it into their best work ever, then submitting it to a contest or a call for writing.

I'd Like to Go Digital

34. Recording/Streaming the Celebration: Recently I received an invitation to a wedding in Lima, Peru, taking place in my hometown. I reread the invitation in order to make sense of it. The couple decided to stream their wedding celebration so friends and family in the States could celebrate with them. There are many family members and friends who would like to join us for a writing celebration but are not able to attend in person. Consider streaming the celebration via Google Hangouts so others can join.

35. Twitter: Students rejoice by sharing on Twitter favorite lines from their classmates' writing. Twitter followers encourage students by responding to these lines.

36. Digital Storytelling: Digital storytelling may sound appealing, but how do you get started? One of my favorite resources is Alan Levine's wiki, *50+ Web 2.0 Ways to Tell a Story*. He updates it regularly and includes dates along with the links to make it user friendly. Inviting just a few students at a time to create a digital story makes it more manageable. So, if you have eight units of study and twenty-four students in your class, then three students would create a digital story each unit.

37. Blog: Scan and share student writing on your classroom blog. For older students, consider creating a blog posting schedule so they can take turns writing posts for the blog.

38. Slice of Life Blogging: Just for the month of March, help older students establish their own blogs and participate in the Slice of Life challenge on the *Two Writing Teachers* blog (Ayres and Shubitz 2013). By blogging, students can connect with other students around the globe. An alternative is to create a classroom Slice of Life blog and have students take turns sharing their slices. For more information, check out the Slice of Life challenge page at *Two Writing Teachers* and check the site each February for more information on that year's challenge. An additional way to rejoice at the end of the month is through a Slice party—serve slices of different kinds of food. Students can bring a favorite slice of writing to the celebration as a means of reflection.

39. Skype: Plan to celebrate with another classroom via Skype. When classrooms are connected via Twitter, blogs, and Facebook, it is only natural to want to see each other "in person." Skype (or Google Hangouts) provides a means for students to meet without getting on a bus. Prior to the celebration, have students generate a list of questions to ask and respond to in order to provide some structure to the celebration.

40. Film Festival: Create a video with iMovie or Windows Movie Maker as a way to share student writing and reflect on the unit of study. Wondering how to make a video? Just search for a tutorial about your program on YouTube. All Macs come with iMovie, and all PCs come with Windows Movie Maker. Trust me, you can do it! Pop popcorn and settle in for the viewing. Bethany Hall uses this kind of celebration as a culminating event in her second-grade classroom. They share research projects, comics, fairy tales, blog posts, narratives, and how-to presentations. Bethany hosts two screenings (Figure 5.17), one during the day and a second in the evening for parents. Check out the way she creates a mood by using red carpet (Figure 5.18) and favors for families to take home (Figure 5.19).

Figure 5.17 Students and families watch a video of students sharing their writing.

Figure 5.18 A red carpet sets the mood for a screening of a video celebration of student writing.

Figure 5.19 Attendees appreciate thoughtful favors like these!

CLOSING THOUGHTS

My husband and I adopted three of our children from the state when they were the ages of four, six, and seven. As they adapt to life as a forever family, our constant conversation has been about making choices and the power we have as individuals to determine the outcome of our lives.

My side of the conversation sounds like this: "You have the power to decide if the day is going to be pleasant. It is completely up to you. You can make choices that lead to a pleasant day or choices that lead to unpleasant consequences. Either way it is up to you."

The same is true in our classrooms. There are many things we cannot control. We cannot control educational mandates. We cannot control fathers drinking and mothers leaving. We cannot control standardized writing assessments.

But we can choose joy.

This is the heart of celebration. We choose joy about the excess periods in a student's writing, because a month ago there were none. We choose joy about the three meager lines of writing, because yesterday there were crushed pencil points and tears. We choose joy about the misspellings, because all of the sight words are accurate.

In the face of so much need, we can make a choice to celebrate. There will always be an error, a refusal, an inadequate paragraph. Student writing will never be perfect. We live among the mess. We can choose to wallow in the doom. Or we can choose joy.

I will always choose joy. I suspect you will too.

BIBLIOGRAPHY

Ayres, Ruth. 2013. *Ruth Ayres Writes* (blog). http://ruthayreswrites.com.

Ayres, Ruth, and Stacey Shubitz. 2013. *Two Writing Teachers* (blog). http://twowritingteachers.wordpress.com/.

Cruz, M. Colleen. 2003. *Independent Writing: One Teacher—Thirty-Two Needs, Topics, and Plans.* Portsmouth, NH: Heinemann.

Kerby, Mona, and Sarah Chauncey. 2013. *Skype an Author Network.* http://skypeanauthor.wetpaint.com/.

Lamott, Anne. 1995. *Bird by Bird: Some Instructions on Writing and Life.* New York: Random House.

Levine, Alan. 2013. 50+ Web 2.0 Ways to Tell a Story. http://50ways.wikispaces.com/.

National Governors Association Center for Best Practices/Council of Chief State School Officers (NGA/CCSSO). 2010. Common Core State Standards. Washington, DC: NGA/CCSSO.

Overman, Christi. 2013. *Superkiddos* (blog). http://www. wearesuperkiddos.blogspot.com/.

Ray, Katie Wood, with Lisa B. Cleaveland. 2003. *About the Authors: Writing Workshop with Our Youngest Writers.* Portsmouth, NH: Heinemann.

Ray, Katie Wood, with Lester L. Laminack. 2001. *The Writing Workshop: Working Through the Hard Parts (And They're All Hard Parts).* Urbana, IL: National Council of Teachers of English.

Yolen, Jane. 2006. *Take Joy: A Writer's Guide to Loving the Craft.* Cincinnati, OH: Writer's Digest Books.